Essential Lives

STEVE JOBS

$\mathcal{S}$TEVE

$\mathcal{J}$OBS

APPLE & IPOD WIZARD

by Scott Gillam

Content Consultant:
Glen D. Sanford, Author & Webmaster
apple-history.com

ABDO
Publishing Company

CREDITS

Published by ABDO Publishing Company, 8000 West 78th Street, Edina, Minnesota 55439. Copyright © 2008 by Abdo Consulting Group, Inc. International copyrights reserved in all countries. No part of this book may be reproduced in any form without written permission from the publisher. The Essential Library™ is a trademark and logo of ABDO Publishing Company.

Printed in the United States.

Editor: Mari Kesselring
Copy Editor: Paula Lewis
Interior Design and Production: Nicole Brecke
Cover Design: Nicole Brecke

Library of Congress Cataloging-in-Publication Data
Gillam, Scott.
  Steve Jobs / Scott Gillam.
      p. cm. — (Essential lives)
  Includes bibliographical references.
  ISBN 978-1-60453-037-7
  1. Jobs, Steven, 1955—Juvenile literature. 2. Computer engineers—United States—Biography—Juvenile literature. 3. Apple Computer, Inc.—History—Juvenile literature. I. Title.

  QA76.2.A2G45 2008
  621.39092—dc22
  [B]
                              2007030837

TABLE OF CONTENTS

Steve Jobs

WHAT MAKES
STEVE JOBS RUN?

A 51-year-old man wearing jeans and a black turtleneck walked confidently to the center of the stage. It was January 9, 2007, and he was about to present a new product from Apple, Inc. The auditorium was filled with 6,000 professionals from the computer industry. Speaking without notes or a speaker's stand, Steve Jobs, Chief Executive Officer (CEO) of Apple, talked for more than an hour about a product that had been developed in great secrecy over a number of months. After introductory remarks, Jobs introduced the product:

> *We're going to make some history here today. ... Today we're introducing three revolutionary new products. The first one is a widescreen iPod with hand controls. The second is a revolutionary mobile phone. And the third is a breakthrough Internet communications device. An iPod, a phone, an Internet mobile communicator. An iPod, a phone, an Internet mobile communicator. Are you getting it?[1]*

The audience was on the edge of their seats in anticipation. Jobs was carefully building the suspense. A graphic cube began to rotate on the huge screen behind him. On

"Talk about hype. In the last six months, Apple's iPhone has been the subject of 11,000 print articles, and it turns up about 69 million hits on Google. Cultists are camping out in front of Apple stores; bloggers call it the 'Jesus phone.' All of this before a single consumer has even touched the thing. ... Unless you've been in a sensory-deprivation tank for six months, you already know what the iPhone is: a tiny, gorgeous hand-held computer whose screen is a slab of touch-sensitive glass."[2]

—David Pogue,
technology columnist for
The New York Times

Steve Jobs presents the iPhone.

three faces of the cube were symbols of the iPod, the phone, and the Internet device. Finally, Jobs announced the new product:

> *These are not three separate devices. This is one device. We are calling it iPhone.*[3]

Jobs's announcement was met with applause. The audience and the press that covered this keynote presentation at MacWorld in San Francisco, California, were excited. The "buzz" over the new iPhone continued for the next six months, even though no iPhones would go on sale until the end of June. No matter how successful the iPhone would prove to be, the sales and marketing effort was unmatched in Jobs's long list of product rollouts, beginning with the highly successful Apple II, the first widely distributed personal computer.

THE SIGNS OF A SUCCESSFUL BUSINESS LEADER

Steve Jobs's presentations mark him as a successful business leader in many ways. He is a master sales representative. His main focus is to demonstrate that his product is better than the others. His commitment to the innovation and excellence of Apple is outstanding. He also is a great product manager because he is completely familiar with all aspects of the product he has developed. And, he is a true believer in his products. Jobs is always filled with enthusiasm,

Demonstrating the iPhone

To illustrate the calling features of the iPhone during the presentation, Jobs placed a call to someone who had worked on the product and who just happened to be in the auditorium audience. Both sides of the seemingly impromptu (but in reality carefully scripted) phone call were heard on speakerphone by the thousands in the auditorium.

at least in public, for each new product he develops. In the competitive technology market, Jobs is a corporate cheerleader for Apple. He acknowledges the success of his main rival, Microsoft, and in the next breath, he criticizes their products as "second-rate" when compared to Apple's user-friendly, sleekly designed goods.

There is one aspect of Jobs's success as a business leader that is harder to define. Many say he has charisma—the personal appeal or charm that inspires employees to walk the extra mile, or walk the extra hour, in order to satisfy their boss. Others disagree, noting that he has been known to reduce employees to tears with his extreme and often

A Corporate Leader at Work

Steve Jobs's keynote speeches may seem informal, but each presentation takes weeks of preparation. Jobs oversees that preparation. First, Jobs reviews each product that might be presented. He chooses only those that he feels are truly ready to present to the public. Then he asks those teams to prepare material that will show how the product works by demonstrating it in a practice session. If Jobs is not happy with the demonstration, he may threaten to pull it from the final program. By the day of the actual presentation, however, everything has been polished to run smoothly. Stage sets have been built, sound and lighting systems checked, and backup systems are in place in case any computer fails. Everything needs to be perfect for the final presentation in front of a live audience.

Although Steve Jobs might seem to be the star of the show, all of his presentations are team efforts. At the end of the keynote speech, Jobs always remembers to acknowledge and thank everyone who worked on the product.

unrealistic demands. Whether one admires his seductive charm or fears his harsh criticism, few would disagree that his ability to command and inspire others has enabled him to become one of the most successful CEOs in the history of the computer industry.

DETERMINATION

Although Jobs is now CEO of Apple, Inc., he was not always so fortunate. In fact Jobs's early career at Apple is littered with failed projects, some of which resulted in expensive losses. He also is known for his arguments with coworkers. But through it all, Jobs has held on to his desire to create and inspire. He was never the type of person to give up once he set his mind to something. His drive to succeed, often only on his own terms, has been the key to his outstanding accomplishments.

Relationship with Coworkers

Not everyone finds it easy to work with Steve Jobs. Apple Chief Scientist Larry Tesler explains Jobs's relationship with his coworkers: "Everyone had been terrorized by Steve Jobs at some point or another. ... But on the other hand, I think there was an incredible respect for Steve Jobs by the very same people."[4]

How did Steve Jobs acquire the skills that made him the highest-paid CEO in the United States in 2006? To begin to answer that question, one has to go back to 1955 and to a little town in California called Mountain View. At that time, the area was known for its fruit orchards. Later, it would become known as Silicon Valley and produce an entirely different kind of product.

"You've got to find what you love. ... The only way to do great work is to love what you do. If you haven't found it yet, keep looking. Don't settle. As with all matters of the heart, you'll know when you find it."[5]

—*Steve Jobs*

The iPhone is displayed on a screen behind Steve Jobs.

Silicon Valley today

YOUNG STEVE JOBS

s a youngster, Steve Jobs was bored by school. He often got into trouble by playing practical jokes on other students or on teachers. Once, he and a friend traded their bike lock combinations with everyone else who biked to school. Then they switched all the bike locks when no one was looking. It took hours for everyone to get their bikes back into action. The prank took skill, attention to detail, and the ability to persuade.

EARLY LIFE

Steve was born on February 24, 1955, in San Francisco to two unmarried graduate students: Joanne Schieble, an American, and Abdulfattah John Jandali, a Syrian. Feeling unprepared to care for the baby, they put him up for adoption. He was adopted by Paul and Clara Jobs of Mountain View, California, and Steve came to think of them as his only parents. A few years later, the Jobs family adopted another child, Patricia. Later, Steve's birth parents would marry and have another child—a fact Steve would only learn much later in his life. Steve's biological mother later had a second child, Steve's sister Mona Simpson.

Neither of Steve's adoptive parents had attended college. Paul Jobs worked at different times

"I was very lucky. My father, Paul, was a pretty remarkable man. He never graduated from high school. He joined the Coast Guard in World War II and ferried troops around the world for General Patton; and I think he was always getting into trouble and getting busted down to private. He was a machinist by trade and worked very hard and was kind of a genius with his hands. ... He spent a lot of time with me ... teaching me how to build things."[1]

—*Steve Jobs*

as a machinist, a used-car salesman, and a real estate broker. He even worked as a repo man and repossessed cars and other items from people who failed to keep up on their payments. At times while raising her children, Steve's mother worked part-time as a payroll clerk. Paul and Clara Jobs loved their children and saved money to fulfill a promise they had made to Steve's birth parents when he was adopted—he would go to college.

ECONOMIC PROBLEMS

Saving money for Steve's college education was not easy for his parents. Steve's father struggled to support his family. Clara took on babysitting jobs to cover Steve's swim lessons. For both parents, young Steve was a special child for whom they were willing to make sacrifices.

In his moonlighting as a car restorer, Paul was good at bargaining to get the lowest price on parts. Steve often joined his father in these sessions and learned a lot that would be useful later in life when he would negotiate with other companies. When Steve's father sold the cars he had restored, he did not always set a price high enough to give him much profit—a problem his son would never have. Fed up with his low wages and unsuccessful car business, Paul switched careers and became a real estate broker. This job paid much better, but he hated the flattery that was necessary to succeed. Paul ended up working as a machinist again for very low wages.

One day in class, perhaps sensing Steve's frustration, his teacher asked him an innocent question, "What is it in this universe you don't understand?" Nine-year-old Steve glumly answered, "Why is my family so broke?"[2]

A Helpful Teacher and Neighbors

Steve was obviously bright. One teacher later remembered how he always had a different way of looking at a problem. His low grades and pranks, however, had gotten his school career off on the wrong foot. Fortunately, Steve's fourth-grade teacher, Mrs. Hill, found a way to motivate him. "I have this math workbook," she said. "If you take it home and finish on your own without any help and you get it 80 percent right, I will give you five dollars and one of these really big suckers."[3] Whether it was the money, the candy, or the attention, Mrs. Hill's proposal

"Steven is an excellent reader. However, he wastes much time during reading period."[4]
—*Steve Jobs's sixth grade report card*

worked. Steve completed the assignment. More importantly, he says, he grew to so respect his teacher that,

> ... it sort of re-ignited my desire to learn. ... I think I probably learned more academically in that one year than I learned in my life.[5]

Steve also learned a lot outside the classroom. His father marked off a section of his workbench for Steve and showed him how to use tools. Steve also was fortunate to grow up in a part of the country that later became known as Silicon Valley. Many engineers lived in the area and worked for electronics companies such as Hewlett-Packard. One of these engineers, Larry Lang, lived near the Jobs family. Through Lang, Steve learned how to build devices such as a ham radio or a hi-fi amplifier and tuner from kits, called Heathkits, sold by the Heath Company in Michigan. As a result, Steve says, he gained "an understanding of what was inside a finished product and how it worked."[6]

"School was pretty hard for me at the beginning. My mother taught me to read before I got to school and so when I got there I really just wanted to do two things. I wanted to read books because I loved reading books and I wanted to go outside and chase butterflies. ... I encountered authority of a different kind ... and I did not like it. And they really almost got me. They came close to really beating the curiosity out of me."[7]

—Steve Jobs

STEVE'S FIRST LOOK
AT A COMPUTER

Steve's curiosity about machines grew when he saw his first computer. This key event occurred at a meeting of a computer club for kids sponsored by Hewlett-Packard. "I was maybe 12," he recalls. "They showed us one of their new desktop computers and let us play on it. I wanted one badly. I thought they were neat."[8] A year later, Steve needed some parts for a project he was building. Perhaps made more confident by his experiences building Heathkits and participating in the computer club, he called Hewlett-Packard's head, Bill Hewlett, and asked for the parts. Impressed by the boy's knowledge and direct approach, Hewlett gave Steve the parts and even offered him a summer job.

BORED AND RESTLESS

For the most part, especially in the classroom, Steve remained bored and restless. He was a loner

Pranks at University of California, Berkeley

One of Steve's practical jokes involved a TV jammer on which he collaborated with his friend, Steve Wozniak. The device consisted of an oscillator that gave off frequencies that would scramble the signals of nearby television sets. As a high school student, Steve recalls going with Wozniak and the oscillator into a dorm at UC-Berkeley, where the older Wozniak was a student. Secretly turning on the machine, they enjoyed annoying the students living there who were trying to watch the latest *Star Trek* episode.

Years later, Steve Wozniak and Steve Jobs would be cofounders of Apple Computer, Inc.

with few outlets for his talents except playing practical jokes. Steve did enjoy swimming and was on the school swim team, but he could not stand to lose a race. One of his classmates later recalled, "He was pretty much a crybaby. He'd lose a race and go off and cry. He didn't quite fit in with everybody else. He wasn't one of the guys."[8] What would it take to unlock the true genius of Steve Jobs and make him one of the leaders of the personal computer revolution?

Steve Meets His Future Business Partner

It was probably inevitable that Steve Wozniak and Steve Jobs would eventually meet. Steve Jobs was five years younger than the fellow genius who would later be nick-named "Woz" (according to Wozniak, this was short for "Wheels of Zeus"). They lived in the same area and shared the same passion for all things electronic. Their mothers met when Wozniak's younger brother Mark swam on the same team as Steve Jobs. But it was Steve's junior high school friend Bill Fernandez who first introduced the two Steves. As Woz describes it in his autobiography, *iWoz:*

> One day Bill told me, "Hey, there's some-one you should meet. His name is Steve. He likes to do pranks like you do, and he's also into building electronics like you are."[9]

The two did indeed have a lot in common, even though Jobs was five years younger than Wozniak. Actually, Jobs knew far less about electronics than Wozniak. The biggest differ-ence between them, however, was that Jobs had a supersized ambition to succeed, while Wozniak's goals—a steady job with creative challenges—were much more modest.

Steve called Bill Hewlett to ask for computer parts.

Steve Wozniak with his son

DROPPING OUT AND
DROPPING IN

S teve Jobs graduated in the spring of 1972 from Homestead High School, one of the best high schools in California. Its location in Silicon Valley and proximity to Palo Alto, home of Stanford University, meant that the area had a steady

crop of bright students. In 1968, the high school had an enrollment of approximately 2,500 students. Many of the students were the sons and daughters of electrical engineers.

This region became known as the birthplace of the modern personal computer. In 1959, Robert Noyce coinvented the integrated circuit, or microchip. In 1968, he founded Intel Corporation, a maker of computer chips. Using Noyce's invention, Ted Hoff, a resident of Sunnyvale, fathered the microprocessor in 1969. Steve Wozniak, who also lived in Sunnyvale, would use those inventions in 1975 to create the first mass-produced personal computer.

Wozniak, whose father was an engineer at Lockheed, was a graduate of Homestead High School. Homestead attracted teachers with a scientific background, such as John McCollum, who taught electronics to budding computer engineers. Wozniak was one of his best pupils. Two years after Wozniak graduated from Homestead, Steve Jobs also became one of McCollum's students. Jobs's

> "I so clearly remember [my father] telling me that ... someone who could make electrical devices that do something good for people takes society to a new level. He told me that as an engineer, you can change your world and change the way of life for lots and lots of people."[1]
> —*Steve Wozniak*

unique way of thinking, however, did not mesh well in the class, and he quit taking courses with McCollum after only a year. Jobs was more of a tinkerer than a dedicated engineer. He was a dreamer and designer rather than a scientist and inventor. But Jobs was learning how to inspire others to carry out his ideas and designs by the force of his personality.

Taking after his father, but focusing on electronics rather than automobiles, Jobs spent much of his free time after school finding sources of computer and stereo parts. Jobs then either sold the parts at a higher price or used them to repair equipment at a profit. He worked summers on a Hewlett-Packard production line making electronic equipment and was able to attend the lectures that Hewlett-Packard offered.

COLLEGE DROP-IN AND DROP-OUT

Despite his family's modest finances, Jobs persuaded his parents to let him apply to Reed

Different Personalities

Steve Jobs and Steve Wozniak complemented each other as work partners because of their different personalities and approaches to running a business. Steve Wozniak explains, "Steve Jobs ... showed me how brave he was by scoring free [computer] chips just by calling sales reps. I could never do that. Our introverted and extroverted personalities (guess who's which) really helped us in those days. What one of us found difficult, the other often accomplished pretty handily."[2]

College in Portland, Oregon—one of the most expensive private colleges in the United States. The small college was known for its emphasis on independent and rigorous thinking. Jobs planned to study literature, philosophy, and physics. Later, perhaps recalling his brief formal college education, Jobs would claim, "I would trade all my technology for an afternoon with Socrates."[3]

Jobs's plans for a college education changed, however, when he enrolled in the fall of 1972 and realized how expensive college was. After six months, he dropped out. Ever the salesman, Jobs talked the dean into letting him continue to live on campus. In addition, he was permitted to sit in

Steve Skirts the Law

Steve Jobs has said that without the support and help of a few teachers and friendly neighbors, he might well have ended up in jail. Perhaps he was remembering the scheme in which he conspired with his older friend Steve Wozniak.

Like many other early hackers, Wozniak was aware of an electronic device called a "blue box." A blue box reproduced the tones once used by the telephone system to route long-distance calls. By dialing a long distance number and reproducing a 2400 Hz whistling sound, the dialer could make a free call. Using the blue box, Wozniak obtained the pope's telephone number, called the Vatican, and asked to speak to the pontiff, who was asleep at the time.

In 1971, Jobs persuaded Wozniak to start a small business selling the illegal devices. Later, however, Jobs had second thoughts about what they were doing and shut the business down.

Dropping in on a calligraphy class similar to this changed Steve's understanding of typefaces and fonts.

on classes. As he later described the decision to drop out, Jobs recalled that,

> *It was pretty scary at the time, but looking back it was one of the best decisions I ever made. The minute I dropped out, I could stop taking the required classes that didn't interest me, and begin dropping in on the ones that looked interesting.*[4]

For Jobs, it was one of the happiest times of his life. He camped out on the dorm room floors of various college friends or in vacant dorm rooms, collected cans to recycle for spending money, and hiked seven miles (11 km) once a week for a free meal at a Hare Krishna temple. Most importantly, he was learning what he wanted to learn at his own pace.

For example, he sat in on a calligraphy class in which he learned different ways to write letters. The class fascinated him. Ten years later, the Macintosh computer was the first to introduce multiple fonts. Jobs credits the calligraphy course at Reed for giving him the idea for the feature. Every personal computer since the Apple has followed its example.

"If I had never dropped in on that [calligraphy] course in college, the Mac would have never had multiple typefaces or proportionally spaced fonts."[5]

—*Steve Jobs*

Although almost two years as a would-be student at Reed College had been stimulating intellectually, Jobs eventually tired of the constant need to come up with cash to survive. During the last six months of his time at Reed College, he moved off campus, rented a room, and took a job maintaining electrical equipment in a lab. He also was reading and meditating in an effort to figure out what to do with his life. He decided to move back in with his parents and look for a job in his old community. He wanted to use his technical skills to make enough money to finance a trip to India, where he hoped to find enlightenment.

In the fall of 1974, Jobs landed a job with Atari. The video game maker ignored Jobs's scruffy appearance and aggressive behavior. Despite his physical appearance and hypercritical attitude, Jobs picked up enough skills to impress his boss. When Atari had a production problem with a game that was shipped to Germany, the company sent Jobs to Europe to fix the glitch. He eagerly took the assignment, mostly because he could visit India on the way home. Yet that visit, and a later one to a commune in Oregon, brought him no closer to finding out what he wanted to do with his life. Jobs was 20 years old and did not know how he was going to make a living.

Jobs had remained friends with his older acquaintance, Steve Wozniak. A lightbulb was about to go off in Wozniak's head that would radically change the direction of the computer industry. And it was Steve Jobs who would be largely responsible for determining the speed and force of that change.

"Thomas Edison did more for the world than all the Eastern religions combined."[6]

—*Steve Jobs*

Steve Jobs visited India in search of enlightenment.

Altair 8800 computer

THE FIRST
APPLE COMPUTER

he first computers filled an entire room and ran on old-fashioned vacuum tubes. By the early 1970s, most computers were still noisy, refrigerator-sized machines. They also needed more than one person to operate them. A programmer would write computer instructions in a programming language or code. Then a keypunch operator would enter these coded instructions onto punch cards. The programmer would use a card reader device to transmit the program from the cards to the computer.

The newer computers ran on transistors rather than vacuum tubes. While they were smaller, they were still cumbersome. The computers were not designed to be operated by a single person. Furthermore, the different parts of any one computer—the processor, the terminals, and the software—were usually produced by different companies.

In 1972, Intel released the first eight-bit microprocessor, the Intel 8008. Two years later, this was followed by the more powerful 8080. The new Intel chips were small, powerful, and cheaper than previous chips. These devices made personal computers possible. Taking advantage of the new technology, the MITS company in Albuquerque, New Mexico, produced the Altair 8800—a desktop

"If the automobile followed the same development cycle as the computer, a Rolls-Royce would today cost $100, get a million miles to the gallon, and explode once a year, killing everyone inside."[1]
—*Robert X. Cringely, author*

computer the size of a microwave oven. The 12-year-old daughter of the editor of *Popular Electronics*, a magazine that featured the new product on its January 1975 cover, suggested the name. It came from the TV series *Star Trek*. The Altair was an immediate success with computer hobbyists.

WOZNIAK FINDS A WAY

Steve Wozniak and Steve Jobs were two of those hobbyists. They both attended informal meetings of a group in the Menlo Park area that became known as the Homebrew Computer Club. The Altair 8800 was demonstrated at Homebrew's first official meeting on March 5, 1975. Wozniak felt out of place at the meeting because he was not familiar with the Intel chips. He had been working on calculators, not computers, for the past three years at Hewlett-Packard. Still, he was curious enough to take the schematic diagrams of the 8800 that were being handed out at the meeting. To his amazement, when he looked at the diagrams, Wozniak found that they were almost the same as those for a computer he had designed with a group of friends almost five years earlier.

"Man is still the most extraordinary computer of all."[2]

—*John F. Kennedy, speech on May 12, 1963*

Inspired by this discovery, Wozniak immediately began to design a desktop computer similar to the Altair that would take advantage of the new 8008 chip. But his vision went further than the Altair, whose switches and lights looked more like the control panel on an aircraft. He envisioned a central processing unit, or CPU, and a video monitor that would display commands that he entered using a keyboard. Wozniak had already designed and built a TV monitor and terminal. He knew programming and had decided that any computer he built would be programmed in BASIC. After reading Bill Gates's BASIC program for the Altair, Wozniak sensed that this would be the computer language of the future. While his previous computer had its CPU on several chips, the Altair's CPU was on a single chip. Wozniak was able to obtain some chips inexpensively through friends at Hewlett–Packard. Working after hours and on weekends at Hewlett–Packard, Wozniak worked

"Here's to the crazy ones. The misfits. The rebels. The trouble-makers. The round heads in the square holes. The ones who see things differently. They're not fond of rules, and they have no respect for the status quo. You can quote them, disagree with them, glorify, or vilify them. But the only thing you can't do is ignore them. Because they change things. They push the human race forward. And while some may see them as the crazy ones, we see genius. Because the people who are crazy enough to think they can change the world are the ones who do."[3]

—"Think Different" commercial run by Apple, Inc.

steadily to make his vision a reality. Finally, after many hours of designing, programming, debugging, and just plain trial and error, Wozniak typed a few letters using the keyboard. He later wrote,

> *I was shocked. The letters were displayed on the screen! … It was the first time in history anyone had typed a character on a keyboard and seen it show up on a screen right in front of them.*[4]

The date was Sunday, June 29, 1975.

In his work, Wozniak used chips that he had obtained through his job or that he could buy from friends. The best chips, made by Intel, were so expensive that he would not even consider them. Then he discussed his work with Steve Jobs. Jobs was able to persuade an Intel representative to donate some of their chips to the project. As Wozniak recalled, "Steve knew how to talk to a sales representative. I could never have done that; I was way too shy."[5] Although the final computer did not end up using the Intel chips, Jobs's ability to promote the project would be crucial to its success.

Wozniak freely shared the schematic diagrams for his new computer with anyone who was interested.

Steve Jobs, however, soon noticed that a few people were actually building the computers themselves. He suggested to Wozniak that they form a company to produce the circuit boards. He determined they could make the boards for $20 and sell them for $40. By investing $1,000, they could double their money. Wozniak was doubtful, but he liked the idea of the two of them owning a company. To raise the cash, Jobs sold his VW van and Wozniak sold his HP-65 calculator. On April 1, 1976, the

Bill Gates and Paul Allen

In Cambridge, Massachusetts, a Harvard upperclassman Paul Allen showed the *Popular Electronics* magazine to his friend, a sophomore named Bill Gates. Both were convinced that personal computers such as the Altair were the way of the future.

Gates called Ed Roberts, the inventor and manufacturer of the Altair, and said he had written a program in BASIC that would run the Altair. Roberts expressed interest. There were only two problems. First, Gates had not written the program yet, though he was confident that he could. Second, Gates and Allen did not have an Altair computer, since none had been produced yet. The picture on the magazine cover only showed the outer shell. There was nothing inside the shell.

Working with the Intel 8008 microprocessor manual and the diagrams published in *Popular Electronics*, Allen was able to adapt the computer in the Harvard lab to work similar to the 8008 chip. Meanwhile, Gates was able to compress the instructions to run the program into a single paragraph. However, Gates and Allen did not know whether the program would really work when tested on an actual machine. Fortunately it did. In that single demonstration, Gates and Allen began a career that would make Gates a multibillionaire and Microsoft a household name.

two young men officially started
their new company. They named it
Apple Computer, since Jobs had just
returned from a farm in Oregon
where he had enjoyed picking apples.
A friend of Jobs from Atari offered
to design a machine-ready circuit
board based on Wozniak's design for
approximately $600.

All the pieces of the Apple
Computer company's plan now
seemed to be in place. Only one
major question remained: Would
anyone buy what they proposed to
produce?

Steve Jobs named his new computer company Apple Computer because he had just returned from a farm where he had picked apples.

Mike Markkula invested in Apple.

APPLE COMPUTER
TAKES OFF

With the Apple circuit board ready to sell, Steve Jobs quickly sprang into action. Following up with the owner of a local computer hobby shop whom he had met through the Homebrew Computer Club, Jobs soon received

an order. The order was for 50
computers. This amounted to
approximately $25,000 in sales
and an estimated profit of $5,000.
However, the shop owner wanted to
sell assembled computers, not just
the circuit boards that Wozniak had
designed. Now Jobs needed to come
up with the parts and find workers to
put the computers together. He found an electronics
distributor in Palo Alto who agreed to sell Jobs
$20,000 worth of parts. Now came the difficult
part. Jobs had only 30 days to assemble and deliver
the 50 finished computers.

"We had quite a few arguments, but I made all the technical decisions. Jobs was basically a scrambler, looking for parts, and running the errands that needed to be done."[7]
—Steve Wozniak

Jobs hired his pregnant sister, Patty, and various
friends to help him assemble the circuit boards.
They set up shop, first in the apartment of
Wozniak's parents, later at Jobs's parents' garage.
Even Jobs's mother helped out by answering the
phone and dealing with visiting salespeople and
suppliers. The team could only deliver 50 completed
circuit boards, rather than finished computers,
at the end of the 30 days. Jobs used his skills of
persuasion, and their customer accepted the goods.
Apple was on its way.

WORMS IN THE APPLE

As exciting as it was to launch their company, the Apple I computer was not a complete success. Prospective buyers were disappointed that it did not use the much-praised Intel 8080 microprocessor. To work properly, the computer also needed various add-ons. This included an interface that would load the BASIC instructions, as well as a reliable power source. This required extra work for the two entrepreneurs.

In addition, new companies began to produce computers to compete with the Apple I. Among the members of the Homebrew Computer Club, the Apple I ranked only eighth in popularity.

A FINANCIAL SAVIOR

Jobs and Wozniak were lucky, however, to win the financial support of Mike Markkula, a marketing genius and venture capitalist.

An Almost–Millionaire

When Apple I was not a complete success, one of the original investors, Ron Wayne, got cold feet and sold his share to Jobs and Wozniak. A few years later, Wayne's share, once worth about $1,700, would have been worth tens of millions of dollars.

Wayne recalls the event: "Steve Jobs was an absolute whirlwind, and I had lost the energy needed to ride whirlwinds. I made the best decision with the information available to me at the time."[2]

Markkula was impressed with the two young men. In return for one-third ownership in the company, he agreed to lend Apple $250,000 to incorporate the business and develop an improved version of the Apple I. He did so only under the condition that Wozniak agree to cut all ties to Hewlett-Packard. Otherwise, Hewlett-Packard could claim the rights to Wozniak's computer inventions. This was a difficult decision for Wozniak, but he eventually agreed. All three partners now decided to hire a fourth person—engineer and executive Michael Scott—to be the president of Apple Computer, since neither Jobs, Wozniak, nor Markkula believed that they had the executive experience to run a company.

Apple Ascending

With the Apple II, introduced in 1977 at a price of $1,295, Apple Computer hit gold. As the first widely marketed, fully programmable, fully assembled desktop computer, it was quite advanced. Beginners as well as experienced users were impressed by Apple II's color graphics, built-in keyboard, speaker, power supply, and casing. Wozniak was the brains behind almost all of the computer's new features. Jobs's part in the triumph was mainly to insist on the highest standards for those working to make the final product. He played a major role in overseeing the design of the circuit board and approving the appearance of the casing.

Jobs also helped design the famous Apple logo: a rainbow-colored apple with a bite (a pun on byte) taken out of it. He was also largely responsible for the impressive appearance of the Apple display at the 1978 West Coast Computer Faire [sic]. Within days, Apple would sell more of its Apple IIs than the Apple I had sold in an entire year.

Playing Games on Computers

Even after desktop computers first came along, action games were still played on hardwired arcade game machines. Established game makers such as Atari did not make computers. Wozniak examined an Apple II prototype to see if he could adapt Atari's best-selling game, Breakout, which he had invented, for the computer. The object of the game was to knock out the bricks in a wall using a ball controlled by paddles. In a half hour, according to his autobiography *iWoz*, he was able to construct a software program that created the bricks, ball, and paddle, the various motions necessary to make the paddle hit the ball at the bricks, and a scoreboard. He then called Jobs over and showed him what he had done. He told Jobs,

> If I had done all these varieties of options in hardware the way it was always done, it would've taken me ten years to do. Now that games are in software, the whole world is going to change.[3]

As usual, Wozniak was right—and not just about playing games on computers. And as usual, Jobs was quick to pick up on the possibilities for a new marketing niche for computers.

As the Apple II became the talk of the computer world, a slow but dramatic change was beginning to take place in the outward appearance of Steve Jobs. Gone were the bare feet and scruffy look. In their place was a still-longhaired, but well-trimmed, hip-looking young man in a suit. Jobs had carefully polled the potential users of the new computer—young and mostly business professionals such as doctors and professors. Now he crafted both the company's advertising and his own personal appearance to appeal to his growing audience. Still alternately kind and cruel to his employees, the new Steve Jobs was becoming a master at creating a vision of himself and his product line that would serve him well in the years ahead.

Instant Millionaires

When Apple Computer went public in 1980, more than 100 individuals became millionaires overnight. Many were Apple employees who had never made more than $40,000 a year.

Yet Apple's growth was due less to Jobs's drive or Wozniak's brilliance than to the business organization created by Michael Scott, the man they had hired as president. Scott realized that in order for Apple to become a publicly owned company, it needed to produce Apple IIs that met consumer needs. It also needed to promote itself more effectively to both the public and to the press and prepare for expansion by seeking out large investors.

Scott's success at all three of these tasks over the next three years set the stage for what might be Jobs's greatest triumph. December 12, 1980, marked the first time shares in Apple Computer were sold on the stock exchange. The stock opened for the day at $22 per share—50 percent more than expected. By the end of the trading day, the stock closed at $29 per share. Steve Jobs's 15 percent share in the company was now worth more than $200 million. It was an unbelievable sum to the young man who only a few years before had been still living with his parents.

"I was worth over a million dollars when I was twenty-three and over ten million dollars when I was twenty-four, and over a hundred million dollars when I was twenty-five, and it wasn't that important because I never did it for the money."[4]

—*Steve Jobs*

Steve Jobs with an Apple II

Apple computers on the manufacturing line

Problems in Paradise

pple Computer faced tough competition when IBM entered the personal computer market in the summer of 1981 with its own personal computer. The IBM PC and its eventual clones soon overtook the Apple II in sales. In its first two and a half years, IBM sold 1 million PCs and captured 30 percent of the PC market. IBM's success put a lot of pressure on Apple, and Steve Jobs, to create new products that could compete with IBM.

Jobs wanted to build a computer that would be easier to use than the Apple II, which still required entering commands using the keyboard. In the fall of 1979, Jobs was part of a group of Apple executives that had toured the research center at Xerox, an Apple investor in nearby Palo Alto. Jobs was excited by what he saw. Instead of users entering typed commands on a keyboard, they used a mouse to point to an object on the screen or an item on a pull-down menu. This system was called a graphical user interface (GUI), and it was very much like the one used on today's computers.

The Apple Lisa Fiasco

Jobs began pouring millions of dollars into developing the Apple Lisa office computer, which was

"Steve [Jobs] had an incredible ability to rally people towards some common cause by painting an incredibly glorious cosmic objective. One of his favorite statements about the Lisa was, 'We'll make it so important that it will make a dent in the universe.'"[1]
—*Trip Hawkins, marketing planning manager for the Apple Lisa*

expected to sell for $2,000. He predicted that this would be the computer to help Apple regain its dominance in the PC market. Jobs's ability to inspire was legendary, but he was not always good at meeting a budget on schedule. The Apple Lisa project went over budget, and Jobs had a hard time meeting its deadlines. Eventually, Apple president Mike Scott removed Jobs from the Lisa group and made him chairman of the board, where he had no day-to-day responsibilities. The Apple Lisa was completed in September 1982 but cost so much money that it was never commercially successful. The Apple Lisa was a failure.

Market Research

It seems that Steve Jobs often relied on his own instincts when deciding how to create products that would be popular with consumers. When asked if he had sought any public input on how to design a new computer, Jobs replied, "Did Alexander Graham Bell do any market research before he invented the telephone?"[2]

Jobs had an ability to persuade others that the impossible was possible. This ability was often referred to, only half-jokingly, as Jobs's "reality distortion field." Jobs could convince anyone of anything. Indeed, Jobs's vision of a new product (such as a music player the size of a pack of gum) often did appear unreal at the time it was proposed. Jobs was lucky he had his "reality distortion field" to convince people to support his ideas. For those who believed in his vision, working for him could be an inspiring experience. However, Jobs tended to criticize or make fun of any person, idea, or action that did not fit his vision of the moment. For this reason, while most employees found him exciting, others found him difficult. Some tried to avoid working with him; others quit the company. Jobs found that his position at Apple isolated him more and more.

AN APPLE NAMED MACINTOSH

Jobs not only had a vision, he also had brilliant employees. One employee, Jef Raskin, designed a computer he called the Macintosh that would employ user-friendly Xerox features such as the mouse and the GUI. Without any market research to prove it, Jobs sensed that the Macintosh would be the computer of the future. After being kicked out of the Apple Lisa project, Jobs decided to make Macintosh his new venture. He gradually took over Raskin's project and transferred many of the graphical features that had been part of the Lisa. While Raskin had envisioned a cheaper Macintosh computer, Jobs's added features increased the price. Still, the Macintosh prototype took only a few weeks to build, and it was twice as fast as the Lisa and cost one-third as much. Jobs now promoted the development of the Macintosh to the point where employees who worked on the Apple II felt ignored. Due partly to Jobs's attitude, Apple Computer soon split into competing sections, each promoting its own products instead of working together as a team.

By 1984, only 19 percent of all PCs were Apples. In addition, the much-praised Macintosh was not selling in the numbers that Apple had anticipated, despite a brilliant marketing campaign that began with the now-famous "1984" commercial first shown at the 1984 Super Bowl. When Apple reported a huge loss for the fourth quarter of 1983, its stock price fell dramatically. Jobs's personal net worth dropped an astonishing $250 million in just a few weeks.

From Sugar Water to Silicon Valley

Realizing that Apple could benefit from an outsider's perspective, Jobs had recruited John Sculley, CEO of

"1984" Commercial

The famous Macintosh "1984" TV ad was first shown during the 1984 Super Bowl. On a giant TV screen, a figure, intended to represent IBM and its clones, addresses a captive audience. Suddenly, a female escapee runs into the room and hurls a huge sledgehammer at the screen, exploding it in one blinding flash, as a voiceover speaks these words: "On January 24th Apple Computer will introduce Macintosh. And you'll understand why 1984 won't be like *1984.*"[3]

Macintosh

Pepsi Co Inc., to become CEO of Apple on April 8, 1983. Unfortunately for Sculley, he arrived just in time to preside over the decline in Apple's fortunes. For a while, Sculley and Jobs seemed to work together well. In June 1985, however, the fighting among Apple groups resulted in Sculley taking away

Steve Jobs, John Sculley, and Steve Wozniak

Jobs's control over the Macintosh division. The reorganization left Jobs with little to do as chairman except attend occasional board meetings and create new ideas for products. This development was a major blow to Jobs, who had always enjoyed being responsible for the day-to-day operations of his current pet project. Frustrated, Jobs thought he could be a better CEO of Apple than Sculley.

He tried to get board members to vote Sculley out of the company. However, Jobs's plan failed. The board would not vote Sculley out and Jobs continued to be chairman with no real role in the company.

Jobs Resigns from Apple

Exiled to an office that he nicknamed "Siberia," separate from the rest of the Apple campus, Jobs pondered his future. After much research and discussion with professors at Stanford University, he decided to start a new company called NeXT. The

Goodbye to Apple

As Steve Jobs prepared to leave Apple in 1985, he stated:

What I'm best at doing is finding a group of talented people and making things with them. I respect the direction that Apple is going in. But for me personally … if there's no place for me to make things there, then I'll do what I did twice before. I'll make my own place. You know I did it in the garage when Apple started, and I did it in the metaphorical garage when the Mac started.

I helped shepherd Apple from a garage to a billion-and-a-half-dollar company. It took a bunch of rambunctious upstarts, working with very little resources but a certain vision and commitment to do it. I'm probably not the best person in the world to shepherd it to a five or ten billion dollar company, which I think is probably its destiny. And so I haven't got any sort of odd chip on my shoulder about proving anything to myself or anybody else. I had ten of the best years of my life, you know, and I don't regret much of anything. I want to get on with my life.[5]

company would produce a computer that could simulate scientific experiments and be used for teaching purposes. Another problem arose, however, when Jobs gave Sculley a list of names of people from Apple that he planned to take with him to start NeXT. Sculley regarded five of these employees as vital to Apple's success. Sculley accused Jobs of deceiving him about his plans and immediately fired the five employees. On September 17, 1985, Steve Jobs officially resigned from Apple.

By resigning from Apple at the age of 30, Steve Jobs ended what many thought was the most productive period of his adult life. He had started a company and watched it grow from almost nothing to a worldwide, multibillion-dollar corporation with thousands of employees. It was difficult to think of him achieving anything else on so grand a scale. Jobs was definitely down, but far from out. Eventually, he would surprise even his harshest critics with the magnitude of his new achievements.

Steve Jobs with the Macintosh

Steve Jobs gives a keynote address as CEO of NeXT computer.

THE NeXT STEP

B y resigning from Apple, Steve Jobs had dramatically cut his ties to the company that had made him famous. Always a moody person, Jobs was depressed for a while, but two facts soon brought his brain back into focus. First, he was now a very rich man who no longer needed the security of a regular paycheck. Even as Apple stock was sinking in value in the months before he left the company, he had been gradually selling his shares. The stock was worth over $200 million now—more than enough to fund another venture. Secondly, Jobs was still attracted to the idea of designing, building, and selling a powerful computer that would dominate the higher education market. This idea also intrigued the five high-level employees he had persuaded to leave Apple to join him in his new company. In January 1986, Jobs founded his new company and named it NeXT Computer.

Jobs claims that he got the idea for a new computer from a lunchtime conversation with the Nobel Prize-winning biochemist Paul Berg. The scientist had described how his experiments with recombining, or modifying, DNA in the lab took a week or more to run. Jobs responded:

Company Secrets

John Sculley, Apple CEO, was angry that Jobs wanted to take the five Apple employees with him to form NeXT. Sculley explained why those employees were so valuable to Apple:

"Together, they knew our internal schedules, our costs, the focus of Apple's next products … how they would be used, and which individuals and universities we would work with to ensure their success. Their accumulated knowledge would give Steve a decided advantage to compete directly with Apple."[1]

Why don't you simulate them on a computer? Not only will it allow you to run your experiments faster, but someday every freshman microbiology student in the country can play with Paul Berg recombinant software.[2]

CONFLICTING MEMORIES

According to Jobs's recollection, Berg was excited by the idea. As Berg recalls the event, however, he dismissed the proposal. He said a computer that could run such simulations would be too expensive for universities to afford, and the software was not sophisticated enough to recreate the experiments.

However, Jobs was sold on his idea for the new computer. It also fit in with his continuing interest in the education market. Jobs wanted to extend his vision of the personal computer to include every level of education from the elementary grades through graduate school.

BURNING THROUGH MONEY

Confident as always that he was right in his view of the future, Jobs started pouring money into his company. He secured offices for the new company on the Stanford University campus. One of his first employees was an interior designer who spent millions gutting and rebuilding the company's headquarters to meet Jobs's high artistic standards. He also paid $100,000 to a famous designer just to design the NeXT logo. Pitching his ideas constantly, Jobs was able to attract the attention of H. Ross Perot, Texas billionaire. After seeing Jobs describe his venture on television, Perot called and offered to become an investor in NeXT. For $20 million, Perot received a 16 percent stake in the company and a seat on the board of directors.

Form Follows Function

Form follows function is an important rule of art that modern designers follow in deciding how to shape objects, including computers. For example, a computer designer will plan a desktop computer so that the form of the keys fits the shape of fingers. Similarly, the designer will plan the monitor so that it can be adjusted to the angle at which it is viewed. For Jobs, however, the physical appearance of an object is important in itself as well as something to be determined by its use. As Jobs explains,

The best companies pay attention to [the principles of art] ... proportion things appropriately, and it seems to pay off for them. I mean, beyond the functional benefits, the aesthetic communicates something about how they think of themselves, their sense of discipline in engineering, how they run their company. ... Let me give you an example from NeXT. We have probably the most automated factory in the world. Our circuit board comes out untouched by human hands. We have a series of sophisticated robots [that come] in different colors, and I wanted them all painted the same color. ... We don't want people to think of the factory as separate islands of automation. We want people thinking of the whole.[3]

Jobs unveils a NeXT computer at a news conference, while NeXT investor H. Ross Perot looks on.

Later, Canon, known for its quality printers, would pay five times that amount for a similar share in the company.

In another quiet victory for Jobs, Apple agreed not to sue NeXT for stealing Apple employees. There was one condition: NeXT agreed to show all its new products to Apple before releasing them in order to make sure NeXT did not steal any trade secrets.

The NeXT Computer Difference

NeXT released the NeXT Cube computer on October 12, 1988. Several features made the computer unusual at the time besides its cube shape. This was the first computer with built-in, CD-quality sound. More importantly, it used object-oriented programming (OOP) instead of the traditional computer languages. OOP was desirable because it splits large programs into small, self-contained parts, which can be reused for future programs. OOP made it easier to make changes to one part of the program without disturbing the rest. Steve Jobs was so excited by OOP that he made a prediction:

> *All software will be written using object-oriented technology some day. You can argue how long it's going to take, who the winners and losers are going to be, but I don't think a rational person will debate its significance.*[4]

All the money and time that was poured into developing the NeXT Cube did not solve some of its basic problems. As Paul Berg had foreseen, the

The NeXT Joke

Three years after its start, NeXT had yet to sell a single product under its own name. Someone joked, "All we've shipped is a T-shirt."[5]

final product, priced at an eye-popping $6,500, was too expensive for the average buyer, whether an individual or university. One reason for the high price was due to Jobs's insistence on putting too much emphasis on the design and appearance of the simple cube structure. The cube shape also made it more difficult to fit in all the parts, which were normally made for a larger, more rectangular-sized case. Jobs had created a computer that, like the Apple Lisa, was just too costly to be successful. By 1990, NeXT created a new version of the NeXT computer called NeXTstation. It was more traditionally shaped, and the color graphics version was an option. Yet, it was still two or three times more expensive, and slower, than computers made by competitors such as Sun Microsystems. In 1992, NeXT sold only 20,000 computers. Apple sold that many in one week. Gradually, Jobs's partners quit NeXT, and the company seemed to be on the verge of closing. For the next few years it struggled along with the help of additional investments by Canon.

Dismissed

After four of the five cofounders of NeXT had quit, Steve Jobs spoke angrily to the rest of his executive staff: "Everyone here can leave—except me."[6]

THE COMEBACK KID

Although NeXT computer was not very popular, its powerful operating system, NeXTSTEP, attracted attention. Jobs made a difficult decision to put time into developing the NeXTSTEP software, and it paid off. Many computer professionals showed interest in NeXTSTEP. For example, in 1990, Tim Berners-Lee chose a NeXT computer to use when he was inventing the computer language that became the basis for the World Wide Web.

By 1996, Apple was looking for an operating system that would help it regain some of the market share it had lost to computers that used Windows. Apple analyzed the software from four different companies, including Microsoft, and chose NeXTSTEP. A major reason for the decision was Jobs's brilliant sales pitch. He argued that the NeXT software was superior and that the

"The only problem with Microsoft is they just have no taste. I don't mean that in a small way. I mean that in a big way, in the sense that they don't think of original ideas and they don't bring much culture into their products. I have no problem with their success—they've earned their success for the most part. I have a problem with the fact that they just make really third-rate products."[7]

—*Steve Jobs*

entire company, including its 300 employees, would be a tremendous asset to Apple.

In December 1996, Apple bought Jobs's proposal and purchased NeXT for $377.5 million in cash and 1.5 million shares in Apple. The cash went to NeXT's investors; the Apple shares, worth over $30 million, went to Steve Jobs. In addition, Apple agreed to hire him back as a "special advisor." There had never been a comeback such as this in the business world. Like the mythical phoenix, Jobs had risen from the ashes of NeXT to return triumphantly to the company that had forced him to resign 11 years earlier.

Steve Jobs with the NeXTstation

Steve Jobs speaks at a Macworld trade show soon after rejoining Apple.

RETURNING TO APPLE

he company that Steve Jobs rejoined in 1997 was in a much weaker position than the one he had left in 1985. In the years between, Microsoft had almost completely taken over the personal computer market by selling its MS-DOS operating system to IBM PC clone users. Apple still controlled a healthy share of the education market, but only one in twenty general computer users owned a Macintosh or an Apple. The company that had created the first widely used desktop computer, the Apple II, and introduced the first graphical user interface, the Macintosh, was now struggling to survive. In 1996, the company lost $1 billion. The company desperately needed new products that would capture the public's attention. As Jobs later explained the situation at Apple during that time:

"You're never really 'in' with Steve. At any moment you can say something that he thinks is stupid and you'll be relegated to bozo status. He believes everyone is expendable. But very few people write off Steve forever. He's such an engaging person that no matter how much he steps on you, you'll come back. He's the most charismatic person I've ever met. ... I love being around Steve because he's the center of the universe—only it's his universe."[2]
—*Heidi Roizen, longtime colleague of Jobs at Apple*

You need a very product-oriented culture, even in a technology company. Lots of companies have tons of great engineers and smart people. But ultimately, there needs to be some gravitational force that pulls it all together. Otherwise, you can get some great pieces of technology all floating around the universe. But it doesn't add up to much.[1]

It soon became clear that Jobs
saw himself as the "gravitational
force" needed to pull the company
out of its slump. On September
16, 1997, only nine months after
his return to Apple as a "special
advisor," Jobs was officially named
interim CEO of Apple. The title was
later to be humorously shortened
to iCEO, imitating the prefix of the
iMac computer that had become so
popular by then.

Regaining Power at Apple

Knowing that he rubbed many
people the wrong way, Jobs worked to
make himself appear less aggressive.
For example, he accepted a salary
of only $1 a year and refused to take
a real title. However, just months
after the NeXT purchase, Jobs had
placed employees from NeXT in
powerful positions at Apple. Few who
knew him doubted that he intended
eventually to take back control of the

"The rewarding thing isn't
merely to start a company
or to take it public. It's
like when you're a par-
ent. Although the birth
experience is a miracle,
what's truly rewarding
is living with your child
and helping him grow
up. The problem with
the Internet craze isn't
that too many people
are starting companies;
it's that too many people
aren't sticking with it.
That's somewhat under-
standable, because there
are many moments filled
with despair and agony,
when you have to fire
people and cancel things
and deal with very dif-
ficult situations. That's
when you find out who
you are and what your
values are."[3]

—Steve Jobs

company. Some employees, remembering the Apple Lisa fiasco, worried about the effect Jobs might have on Apple as he gained more power. Many employees avoided him, since one of his methods of making Apple successful again was by firing people to save money. On March 14, 1997, Apple fired 4,100 employees—31 percent of its workforce. Apple also dropped a number of its projects, notably the Newton PDA, or personal digital assistant, which had pioneered the recognition of handwriting.

Apple and the Internet

The prefix "i" in Apple products originally stood for Internet, indicating the huge new importance of this resource for all computer users. The Internet was first conceived as a way for U.S. scientists to catch up with the Soviets by sharing information more easily. Universities, the National Science Foundation, and the U.S. Department of Defense all helped in creating networks for sharing information that eventually evolved into the Internet.

In 1990, Tim Berners-Lee figured out how to transmit content over the Internet, thus creating the World Wide Web. The first Web page went online August 6, 1991. Berners-Lee was a British citizen working in the CERN nuclear research firm in Switzerland. In his work, Berners-Lee would receive information over the Internet that was written in many different computer languages on many different kinds of computers. He often had to translate the information so that it could be read by his computer. One day he wondered, "Can't we convert every information system so that it looks like part of some imaginary information system which everyone can read?"[4] Berners-Lee created a computer language that would allow text and images to be hosted on one computer but displayed on another. The result was the World Wide Web.

The iMac was the fastest-selling PC in history.

APPLE AND MICROSOFT MAKE A DEAL

Microsoft and Apple had been fierce competitors and had spent years entangled in various lawsuits.

Apple claimed that Microsoft developed its Windows interface with information it had gained from its access to the Macintosh in its early development. Jobs now sealed a deal with his old rival that some said gave away the Apple "family jewels." In return for being allowed to continue to use the Apple-inspired graphic user interface, Microsoft agreed to invest $150 million in Apple and write Microsoft programs that were compatible with the Macintosh. Jobs also agreed to install the Microsoft Internet Explorer Web browser on all new Macintosh computers. Again, many Apple fans were shocked, but the business community recognized the wisdom of Jobs's deal. Apple stock rose sharply after the agreement was announced and would continue to rise over the next two years.

THE iMAC PHENOMENON

The rise in Apple's fortunes was also due to the phenomenal success of the iMac, first introduced on August 15, 1998. Even before it was available in stores, the original iMac, an egg-shaped model enclosed in plastic, had more than 150,000 preorders.

"We have to let go of the notion that for Apple to win, Microsoft needs to lose. The era of competition between Microsoft and Apple is over, as far as I'm concerned."[5]

—Steve Jobs, introducing Microsoft CEO Bill Gates to the 1997 Macworld Expo

Jobs shows off the iBook.

With its striking design and brilliant advertising campaign, the iMac became the fastest-selling PC in history. Over two million iMacs were purchased in a little more than one year. Adding to the success was that for many buyers, this was either their first computer, or at least their first Apple computer. Finally, Jobs had overseen the creation of a computer that was both popular and affordable.

Features of the iMac

Shunning the beige metal boxes that had typically housed PCs, the iMacs came in a range of colorful plastic cases. The iMac was also the first Macintosh computer to include a universal serial bus (USB). This was a risk for Apple because the USB differed from the serial ports included on previous Apple computers. However the USB enabled the iMac to easily connect to peripherals, such as printers. Since many PCs already had USB ports, hardware makers could now make their products compatible with both PCs and Macs.

Power Macs and Apple Stores

To complete Jobs's strategy to revive Apple, new products began to appear. In addition, a nationwide chain of Apple stores—eventually numbering more than 170—sold, demonstrated, and repaired Apple products. The Power Macintosh had been around since 1994. On November 10, 1997, the Power Macintosh G3 was introduced. It was intended for business and creative

> "At Apple [Jobs] had a difficult time hearing what he didn't want to hear. Now, he's very much more open. He'll say, 'Don't tell me what I want to hear. Tell me the truth.' In reality, it's not always so clear-cut. But he's trying so much harder."[6]
> —*Tom Carlisle, who worked with Jobs at Apple, NeXT, and Pixar*

professionals. It became an immediate success at
the high end of the performance spectrum. For
example, the Power Mac G4's 500-MHz processor
was so powerful that it was classified as a weapon by
the U.S. government. Much of the success of the
powerful G4 was due to Jobs's marketing talent.
Clearly the days of the Apple Lisa and the NeXT
Cube were over for Jobs. In July of 1999, the iBook,
a portable iMac with a wireless networking option,
was introduced with a preorder success of 140,000
orders.

With Apple's profits up, its product line
increasing, and its smaller workforce more efficient,
the announcement at the annual Macworld Expo
on January 26, 2000, was almost anticlimactic.
Steve Jobs was now officially CEO of Apple and
no longer its iCEO. He was back in charge of the
company that he had helped transform over two years
from a weak company to one poised for yet another
breakthrough. ⌐

Steve Jobs poses with the iMac.

Pixar Animation Studios

Pixar Story

During Steve Jobs's 11-year exile from Apple, he started NeXT Computer. He also entered the movie business through the purchase of a small company called The Graphics Group in the Bay Area. Jobs purchased this company for less than $10 million in February 1986 and renamed it Pixar. It had been a division of George Lucas's company, Industrial Light and Magic, which had created special effects for some of the *Star Wars* films. The Graphics Group originally included Ed Catmull, who had a doctorate in physics, and Alvy Ray Smith, a mathematician and economist. Smith had worked briefly at the Xerox PARC facility, where research on the graphic user interface and mouse had so impressed Jobs in 1979.

A New Way of Doing Animation

Before computer animation, each frame of an animated film had to be separately drawn and colored by hand. Since 24 frames per second pass through a movie projector, a full-length feature film such as Walt Disney's *Fantasia* could contain hundreds of thousands of frames that might take hundreds of hours to produce. With computers, these frames could be created and altered quickly. Computer animation not only saves time and money, it also makes more sophisticated types of animation possible. Sometimes the resulting animated figures are almost impossible to distinguish from real people and objects.

Jobs first heard about Ed Catmull and Alvy Ray Smith in 1984. Jobs inspected Catmull and Smith's operation and was amazed at the quality of their computer graphics. Fortunately for Jobs, the two men were looking for a buyer for their division, which had been unsuccessful in breaking into the animated feature film business. For all of their brilliant special effects, the computer they used, which cost $135,000, not counting software, was too expensive for motion picture studios to buy. Since the real money in animation is in making full-length

The Pixar Work Environment

Most companies that make movies operate on a project basis. Directors, actors, producers, and technicians come together to do a film but separate when the film is finished. Pixar hires its employees for the long term so they can develop team relationships and increase their skill level from project to project. Pixar focuses on its employees as well as its projects. Making movies is stressful and expensive. Many things can go wrong in the production process. Pixar reduces the stress by encouraging workplace equality and allowing employees to take courses on company time to improve their skills. The courses are taught at their company-run training program called Pixar University. Any employee may take up to four hours a week of courses that range from comedy improvisation to the use of lighting in movies. Industry analyst Andrew Slabin says,

What makes a movie successful is not only the technology but the story that brings people in to see it over and over. It's got to be edgy, heartfelt, warm. That's what the Pixar movies do. The culture of the firm teaches you to be better at doing that stuff, and [Pixar] University is central to that culture.[1]

animated feature films, Catmull and Smith had to get by doing TV commercials and special effects.

PURCHASING AND PROMOTING PIXAR

After the sale of his Apple stock, Jobs had money to spend. When he bought what would become Pixar, it was agreed that Jobs would own 92 percent of the company, and Catmull and Smith would own only about 8 percent. Jobs, however, wanted to have only limited control of the day-to-day workings of the firm. As principal owner, Jobs first tried to sell the company's main asset, its expensive movie-making computer, in two markets: hospitals and the intelligence community. These kinds of organizations required powerful computers to interpret graphics such as X-rays and satellite photographs. Most potential customers, however, found the computers too complicated to learn how to operate. Eventually Jobs agreed to sell the hardware aspects of Pixar for several million dollars in order to focus on creating software that would generate animated film.

"[Pixar is] a tight-knit company of long-term collaborators who stick together, learn from one another and strive to improve with every production."[2]
—New York Times reporters William C. Taylor and Polly LaBarre on the Pixar culture

Pixar was still losing money, as was NeXT, where Jobs remained even as his original partners gradually left. The only thing that kept him from closing Pixar was that every few years, one of their animated short films would receive an award. In 1986, the animated short *Luxo Jr.* was nominated for an Academy Award. In 1989, *Tin Toy* won an Oscar as the best animated film. These awards showed Jobs that the company had the potential to make money. While the awards were great for the company's reputation, they did not cover the bills. Worth over $200 million when he left Apple in 1985, Jobs had pumped so much money into NeXT and Pixar that he was down to his last $25 million when fortune again smiled on him.

> "I'd watch him address our employees, and the look in their eyes was love. He'd have them twisted around his finger. He's seductive to the nth degree . ... I used to love to see him enter a roomful [sic] of strangers and just take it. Steve has that talent. I think that it's the talent of the tongue."[3]
> —*Alvy Ray Smith, cofounder of Pixar*

A Change in Luck

Impressed with Pixar's work, Disney offered the company a $26 million contract in 1991 to make five computer animated feature films. It was a turning point for Pixar.

In that year, Jobs's personal life also took a turn for the better.

A longtime bachelor, Jobs married Laurene Powell, a graduate student at Stanford. They were married in Yosemite National Park with just a small group of friends attending the ceremony. The couple went on to have three children. Those who knew him during his bachelor days have a hard time believing that Jobs has become a family man. However, those who know him now say that it is true.

Another bright spot in Jobs's changing fortunes was the Computer Animation Production System (CAPS) software package developed jointly by Pixar and Disney. Beginning with *Beauty and the Beast* in 1991, CAPS was used on a series of successful Disney films, including *Aladdin* (1992), *The Lion King* (1994), and *Pocahontas* (1995). Pixar won a technical Academy Award in 1992 for CAPS and another in 1993 for its RenderMan software. RenderMan enabled computers to provide an exact model on film of a setting or character, including color, texture, and lighting. RenderMan is also the most widely used software program in the film industry for creating special effects. It has been used on the great majority of recent films nominated for Academy Awards in the best visual effects category.

THE TRIALS OF *Toy Story*

With a big contract under its belt, Pixar was determined to produce a winning computer-animated feature film. Production on *Toy Story* began on January 19, 1993. Unfortunately, the original script for *Toy Story*, developed mainly by Pixar creative head John Lasseter, had problems. The movie was meant to appeal to children, but the script was more like an adult action movie than the kind of lighthearted story that children prefer. Disney laid off workers and shut down production of *Toy Story* while Pixar came up with a solution to the problem. At an earlier time in his career, Jobs might have thrown a tantrum and demanded the production go forward. Now, however, he was wiser. With no previous experience in the movie business, Jobs realized that the Disney team knew much more than he did about how to develop a script

Laurene Powell Jobs

In addition to helping raise their three children, Laurene Powell Jobs is a company chief and cofounder of two companies in her own right. With a BA and BS from the University of Pennsylvania and an MBA from Stanford, Laurene worked for Merrill Lynch and Goldman Sachs and cofounded a natural foods company. Currently, she is cofounder and president of the board of College Track. This after-school program provides support to high school students who need help in preparing for college.

and plan its production. Jobs would have to wait it out. Lasseter and his team added some scenes to make the main character more lovable, and production resumed.

PIXAR GOES PUBLIC

Toy Story went on to become the most successful animated feature film ever made, earning more than $400 million. Its release on November 2, 1995, was timed not only to take advantage of the winter holiday audiences, but also to precede Pixar's going public and selling shares in its stock. On the first day of trading, the stock price more than doubled. Jobs was now, at least for the moment, officially a billionaire. When Disney bought Pixar on May 5, 2006, Jobs became Disney's largest single shareholder.

Followed by his triumphant return to Apple in 1996, Jobs seemed to be on a roll.

Toy Story

Disney's *Toy Story* tells the tale of a boy named Andy whose toys come alive on his birthday. The toys fear that Andy will get a new toy for his birthday that he will prefer over them. The main conflict in the story is between Woody, a cowboy doll, and Buzz Lightyear, an astronaut doll. Actors whose voices are featured in the film include Tom Hanks, Tim Allen, Don Rickles, and Wallace Shawn.

Steve Jobs had now proved himself a master of
two different industries—computers and movies. It
was hard to imagine him extending his reach into yet
another field, but he was not finished in his quest
for new challenges. His next big idea would prove to
be music to his ears.

John Lasseter holds up two characters from Toy Story.

Steve Jobs presents a new iPod model.

The Age of iPod

espite his success at reviving the Macintosh line with the iMac, Jobs recognized that Apple Computer needed to extend its product line into new areas. Computer technology was changing the world and Apple needed to keep up with the changes. Apple had spent a lot of money developing a PDA called the Newton, but this type of device did not catch Jobs's attention. Music, however, was a different story. Jobs recognized a larger market for music than PDAs. He explains,

> I started asking myself, how useful are [PDAs], really? How many people at a given meeting show up with one? I don't think early cultures had organizers, but I do know they had music. It's in our DNA. [1]

Jobs recognized the importance of music and went to work on tapping into the music market.

DEVELOPING THE iTUNES SOFTWARE

With the development of new computer technologies, music lovers found a way to transfer their music onto computers. They used their computers to convert a CD into a digital MP3 file that could be played

"Music is so deep within all of us, but it's easy to go for a day or week or month or year without really listening to music. The iPod has changed that for millions of people, and that makes me really happy, because I think music is good for the soul." [2]

—*Steve Jobs*

right off the user's computer. Various software programs were available to make these conversions. The best of these programs was SoundJam MP, marketed by Cassidy & Green (C&G), a company that already had close ties to Apple. Apple bought the rights to the SoundJam product code, then hired four of C&G's key employees. C&G soon went out of business, and Apple had a new product—iTunes. The iTunes program could copy, select, and play tracks from a CD as MP3 files on their computers. When Jobs announced the new iTunes program at the Macworld convention on January 9, 2001, the response was enthusiastic. Apple had joined what Jobs called the "digital music revolution."

The iPod Difference

Now that Apple had a superior MP3 program, it needed a winning MP3 player. The existing MP3 players were not very popular. They were not easy to use, had weak batteries, and held relatively few songs. Jobs knew that if he could produce a better MP3 music player, he could not only expand Apple's product line but also create a significant market for downloaded music files.

Tony Fadell, an independent computer hardware developer, had already developed a music player for just such a market. Fadell was glad to sign on with Apple, even though Jobs gave him less than a year to produce a final product. To save time, the production team used existing components such as computer chips and hard drives rather than designing their own. The product had to meet Jobs's high standards, including simple integration with iTunes and no more than three pushes of button to get to a specific song.

The resulting product, the iPod, was introduced on October 23, 2001. After a slow start, sales were phenomenal. As the iPod's popularity increased, Apple created the music player in different styles and forms,

What Does MP3 Mean?

MP3 was first developed by the Motion Picture Experts Group (MPEG), a group of European engineers working to develop standards for translating sounds and pictures into digital format. The project was financed by the European Union beginning in 1987. MP3 is short for MPEG-1 Audio Layer 3. Engineers from five European countries developed MP3 as a way to reduce the amount of data needed to represent an audio recording and still have it sound like a very good reproduction of the original sound. The engineers were able to compress the data representing the sound mainly by eliminating very high and very low sounds. The listener cannot hear these sounds because they are outside the normal hearing range.

Beginning in early 1995, MP3 files began to circulate on the Internet because they could be played on any computer.

including iPod Shuffle, iPod mini, and iPod nano. Many of the new iPods came in a variety of colors and were small enough to fit in a pocket. By 2007, approximately 100 million iPods had been sold. It was the fastest selling music player in history.

Making Copying Music Legal

Apple's iTunes was not the only program taking advantage of the popularity of MP3 music files. Napster, a file-sharing company founded by another college dropout Shawn Fanning had attracted 32 million users in only one year. Napster allowed users to share and download MP3s. There was only one problem—some of these users were breaking the law. By copying music that they had not legally purchased, they were stealing both from the music publishers, who needed to make a profit in order to survive, and from the recording artists, who depended on royalties from their recordings.

To use iTunes technology to distribute music legally, Jobs had to get the five major record companies—Sony, Warner, Universal, EMI, and

"I spent the entire afternoon the other day ... just listening to all my songs in alphabetical order so I'd have no idea what was coming next and it was amazing. It's the greatest invention of the 21st century!"[3]

—David Thewlis, who plays Remus Lupin in two Harry Potter movies

An iPod advertisement

BMG—to agree to let iTunes distribute their music over the Internet. Together, these five companies controlled the rights to the great majority of the popular music in the world. Normally, one would not expect the record companies to be enthusiastic about signing any agreement that could weaken their

> "Stealing music is a behavioral problem more than a technological problem. We believe most people are honest and want to pay for their music."[4]
>
> —*Steve Jobs*

control over the distribution of the music they owned. But these were not normal times. File-sharing services such as Napster, whether legal or not, were threatening the recording business. CD sales were dropping as more and more people shared MP3 files that they had downloaded. Pursuing those who had downloaded music in court was costly as well as unpopular with some consumers. The recording business needed a way to control distribution.

STRIKING A DEAL WITH THE RECORDING COMPANIES

With this threat facing them, and impressed by Jobs's knowledge of music and computers, executives of all five major recording companies eventually agreed to distribute their copyrighted songs. As part of the deal, Apple promised to use digital rights management (DRM) to keep the music from being shared illegally. DRM coded music so that the recording companies could ensure that their music could not be transferred from the buyer's computer to someone else's computer. Music fans could either legally copy many CD tracks or download a large group of music files from the Internet onto their computers. The iTunes software that they used could be downloaded for free.

Apple would pay the recording companies a fee in return for the right to distribute their music to MP3 players via the Internet. For its part, Apple would charge a fee of 99 cents for each song and $9.99 for each album. Consumers could download their music choices from the online iTunes Music Store. The iTunes Music Store was a "digital hub" that Apple created on April 28, 2003, to display its musical and video offerings. The resulting sales have more than confirmed Jobs's hunch that music lovers would embrace the new music distribution system. As of January 2007, iTunes had sold more than 2 billion songs. Approximately 5 million songs a day were being downloaded.

An important milestone in the history of Apple Computer occurred in 2006. For the first time, Apple's profits from its music business were greater than its profits from its computer products. In only three months, Apple sold more than $3 billion worth of iPods, accessories,

"This stuff doesn't change the world. It really doesn't. ... Technologies can make it easier, can let us touch people we might not otherwise. But it's a disservice to constantly put things in a radical new light that it's going to change everything. Things don't have to change the world to be important."[5]

—*Steve Jobs*

and music downloads from its iTunes Music Store.
By comparison, during the same period, Apple
sold $2 billion worth of Macintosh computers.
Recognizing the importance of this significant shift
in its business, Steve Jobs soon announced that
Apple Computer was dropping the word *computer*
from its name. Going forward, the company would
be known as Apple, Inc.

WHERE WILL APPLE LAND NEXT?

With the success of the iPod and iTunes, Jobs
has managed to make dramatic changes in three
different industries: computers, movies, and music.
He achieved all these changes by the relatively young
age of 50. In 2007, with an annual compensation of
$647 million, he was named the highest paid CEO
in the United States by *Forbes* magazine. Though he
has many years left in his working life, it is hard to
imagine how he could move beyond the milestones
he has already passed. No one who has followed his
rapid progress so far, however, would be surprised to
see further changes in store.

Jobs continues to move Apple, Inc. forward.

TIMELINE

1955	1972	1972
On February 24, Steve Jobs is born in San Francisco and is soon adopted by Paul and Clara Jobs.	Jobs graduates from Homestead High School in Cupertino in the spring.	Jobs enters Reed College in Portland, Oregon, but drops out after one semester.

1976	1977	1980
Jobs starts Apple Computer Co. with Steve Wozniak with $1,300 on April 1.	Apple II is introduced in April at a price of $1,295.	On December 12, Apple Computer, Inc. goes public, making Jobs an overnight multimillionaire.

1974

Jobs returns to California and takes a job as a technician with Atari.

1975

The Homebrew Computer Club meets on March 5; the new Altair personal computer is demonstrated.

1975

On June 29, Steve Wozniak successfully tests what would later become the Apple I.

1983

John Sculley, former CEO of Pepsi Co., Inc. becomes Apple CEO on April 8.

1984

Apple Computer introduces the first Macintosh computer on January 24.

1985

Jobs resigns from Apple on September 17.

TIMELINE

1986	1986	1988
In January, Jobs starts NeXT Computer.	Jobs buys The Graphics Group from Lucasfilm for less than $10 million and renames it Pixar.	On October 12 Jobs releases the NeXT Cube at a cost of $6,500.

1998	1999	2000
On August 15, Apple introduces the iMac, which becomes the fastest-selling PC ever: Five million were sold by April 2001.	Apple introduces the iBook on July 21.	On January 5 Jobs accepts the title of CEO of Apple, dropping the "interim."

1991

Jobs marries Laurene Powell on March 18.

1996

In December, Apple buys NeXT and rehires Jobs as a consultant.

1997

On September 16, Jobs becomes Apple interim CEO.

2001

Apple introduces the iPod portable music player on October 23.

2003

On April 28, Apple introduces the iTunes Music Store. By July 2004, more than 100 million songs were sold.

2007

Apple introduces the iPhone on January 9. Apple Computer changes its name to Apple, Inc.

Essential Facts

Date of Birth

February 24, 1955

Place of Birth

San Francisco, California

Parents

Joanne Schieble and Abdulfattah John Jandali (birth parents)
Paul and Clara Jobs (adoptive parents)

Education

Homestead High School; Reed College

Marriage

Laurene Powell (March 18, 1991)

Children

Three children

Career Highlights

Steve Jobs and Steve Wozniak formed their own company, Apple Computer, on April 1, 1976. On December 12, 1980, Apple Computer went public, and Jobs became a multimillionaire overnight. In 1985, Jobs resigned from Apple. In 1997, he rejoined the company. In 1998, Apple launched the iMac. In 2001, Apple released the iPod. In 2007, the iPhone hit the market.

Societal Contribution

Steve Jobs developed new computer technologies and helped make the computer a household item.

Conflicts

In the beginning, Apple struggled to produce a popular computer. The first Apple computer, Apple I, was not a complete success. Once Apple was well established, Jobs attempted to create an office computer called Apple Lisa, but the cost to produce it was too great. Jobs's sometimes negative attitude toward his employees often got in the way of his success.

On September 17, 1985, Jobs resigned from Apple. After leaving Apple, Jobs's new company, NeXT Computer, struggled to produce affordable computers.

Quote

"Innovation distinguishes between a leader and a follower."
—*Steve Jobs*

ADDITIONAL RESOURCES

SELECT BIBLIOGRAPHY

Butcher, Lee. *Accidental Millionaire: The Rise and Fall of Steve Jobs at Apple Computer*. New York: Paragon, 1988.

Deutschman, Alan. *The Second Coming of Steve Jobs*. New York: Broadway, 2000.

Jobs, Steve. "Interview." Computerworld Honors Program International Archives. http://www.cwhonors.org/archives/histories/jobs.pdf.

Malone, Michael S. *Infinite Loop: How Apple, the World's Most Insanely Great Computer Company, Went Insane*. New York: Doubleday, 1999.

Wozniak, Steve, with Gina Smith. *iWoz: Computer Geek to Cult Icon: How I Invented the Personal Computer, Co-founded Apple, and Had Fun Doing It*. New York & London: Norton, 2006.

Young, Jeffrey S., and William L. Simon. *iCon: Steve Jobs, the Greatest Second Act in the History of Business*. Hoboken, NJ: Wiley, 2005.

FURTHER READING

Aaseng, Nathan. *Business Builders in Computers*. Minneapolis, MN: Oliver, 2000.

French, Laura. *Internet Pioneers: The Cyber Elite*. Berkeley Heights, NJ: Enslow, 2001.

Young, Jeffrey. *Forbes Greatest Technology Stories: Inspiring Tales of the Entrepreneurs and Inventors Who Revolutionized Modern Business*. Hoboken, NJ: Wiley, 1998.

Web Links

To learn more about Steve Jobs, visit ABDO Publishing Company on the World Wide Web at **www.abdopublishing.com**. Web sites about Steve Jobs are featured on our Book Links page. These links are routinely monitored and updated to provide the most current information available.

Places to Visit

The Computer History Museum
1401 Shoreline Boulevard, Mountain View, CA 94043
650-810-1010
www.computerhistory.org/about_us.html
This museum contains one of the largest collections of computing artifacts in the world.

U.S. Patent and Trademark Office Museum
600 Dulany Street, Alexandria, VA 22314
571-272-0095
www.uspto.gov/web/offices/ac/ahrpa/opa/museum
Learn about the patent and trademark
systems through various permanent and changing exhibits.

The University of Virginia Computer Museum
151 Engineers Way, Charlottesville, VA 22904
434-982-2200
www.cs.virginia.edu/brochure/museum.html
This museum displays various computer-related artifacts, including the Altair 8800, to help you learn about the history of computers.

GLOSSARY

BASIC
Beginner's All-purpose Symbolic Instruction Code, a computer language invented in 1964.

byte
Eight bits of computer data that together represent a character, number, or color.

central processing unit (CPU)
The computer part that controls and executes operations.

digital rights management (DRM)
The system of coding music and videos so their use can be restricted to certain players or computers.

entrepreneur
Someone who starts businesses and is good at finding new ways to make money.

graphical user interface (GUI)
Pictures (or icons) on a computer screen that represent a program or file. By clicking a mouse on the icon, a computer user can open the program or file.

hardware
The physical parts of a computer, such as the hard drive, monitor, printer, and discs.

integrated circuit
A microchip; an electronic circuit, usually etched on a tiny silicon chip, which can hold thousands of electronic items such as transistors and resistors.

microprocessor
The central processing unit of a computer that interprets computer program instructions and processes data.

MP3
A method of converting sound and video into digital format.

object oriented programming (OOP)
Programming languages such as Java that are organized around objects rather than actions and data rather than logic.

operating system (OS)
> The master software program that manages a computer by controlling input and output to and from its various components.

peripheral
> A piece of computer hardware that connects to a computer such as a printer or a disk drive.

program
> A set of instructions that tells a computer what to do.

software
> A program, or set of instructions, that controls the operation of a computer.

transistor
> A switch in a microchip that controls the output of electricity.

universal serial bus (USB)
> A collection of wires that allows computers to exchange data with external devices.

World Wide Web (WWW)
> A system for linking multimedia documents and displaying them on the Internet.

SOURCE NOTES

Chapter 1. What Makes Steve Jobs Run?

1. Steve Jobs. "Keynote Address," Macworld San Francisco. 9 Jan. 2007. 8 May 2007 <http://events.apple.com.edgesuite.net/j47d5200/event/>.

2. David Pogue, "The iPhone matches most of its hype," *New York Times*. 27 June 2007. 2 July 2007 <http://www.nytimes.com/2007/06/27/technology/circuits27pogue.html>.

3. Steve Jobs. "Keynote Address," Macworld San Francisco. 9 Jan. 2007. 8 May 2007 <http://events.apple.com.edgesuite.net/j47d5200/event/>.

4. "The Steve Jobs way: A relentless pursuit of perfection." CNN. 31 Oct. 2005. 6 July 2007 <http://www.cnn.com/2004/WORLD/americas/04/16/jobs>.

5. "A design, a dream." *U.S. News & World Report*. 31 Oct. 2005. 6 July 2007 <http://www.usnews.com/usnews/news/articles/051031/31jobs.htm>.

Chapter 2. Young Steve Jobs

1. Steve Jobs. "Oral History." Computerworld Honors Program International Archives, 3. 20 Apr. 1995. 30 Mar. 2007 <http://www.cwhonors.org/archives/histories/jobs.pdf>.

2. Michael S. Malone. *Infinite Loop: How Apple, the World's Most Insanely Great Computer Company, Went Insane.* New York: Doubleday, 1999. 10.

3. Steve Jobs. "Oral History." Computerworld Honors Program International Archives, 3. 20 Apr. 1995. 30 Mar. 2007 <http://www.cwhonors.org/archives/histories/jobs.pdf>.

4. Lee Butcher. *Accidental Millionaire: The Rise and Fall of Steve Jobs at Apple Computer.* New York: Paragon House, 1988. 15.

5. Ibid.

6. Ibid.

7. Ibid. 4.

8. Jeffrey S. Young. *Steve Jobs: The Journey Is the Reward.* Glenview, IL: Scott, Foresman, 1988. 21.

9. Steve Wozniak with Gina Smith. *iWoz: Computer Geek to Cult Icon: How I Invented the Personal Computer, Co-founded Apple, and Had Fun Doing It.* New York: Norton, 2006. 88.

Chapter 3. Dropping Out and Dropping In

1. Steve Wozniak with Gina Smith. *iWoz: Computer Geek to Cult Icon: How I Invented the Personal Computer, Co-founded Apple, and Had Fun Doing It.* New York: Norton, 2006. 17.

2. Ibid. 71.

3. "The Classroom of the Future." *Newsweek.* 29 Oct. 2001. 20 Mar. 2007 <www.highbeam.com/doc/1G1-79408808.html>.

4. Steve Jobs. "'You've got to find what you love,' Jobs says." Stanford Report. Online text of Commencement address. Stanford University, 12 June 2005. 20 Mar. 2007 <http://news-service. stanford.edu/news/2005/june15/jobs-061505.html>.

5. Ibid.

6. Jeffrey Young, *Forbes Greatest Technology Stories.* New York: Wiley, 1998. 177.

Chapter 4. The First Apple Computer

1. Robert X. Cringely [Mark Stephens and others writing in *Info-world*]. 28 Mar. 2007 <http://www.sysprog.net/quotes.html>.

2. John F. Kennedy. "Speech." Famous Quotes Page. 21 May 1963. 23 Mar. 2007 <http://www.2-sir.com/CyberSite2/Quotes.html >.

3. "Think Different." advertisement. 1997. 28 Mar. 2007 <http:// pine.psych.cornell.edu/misc/inspirational_quotes.txt>.

4. Steve Wozniak with Gina Smith. *iWoz: Computer Geek to Cult Icon: How I Invented the Personal Computer, Co-founded Apple, and Had Fun Doing It.* New York: Norton, 2006. 166.

5. Ibid. 170.

6. Ibid. 172.

Chapter 5. Apple Computer Takes Off

1. Lee Butcher. *Accidental Millionaire.* New York: Paragon, 1988. 64.

2. Jeffrey S. Young and William L. Simon. *iCon: Steve Jobs, The Greatest Second Act in the History of Business.* Hoboken, NJ: Wiley, 2005. 45.

3. Steve Wozniak with Gina Smith. *iWoz: Computer Geek to Cult Icon: How I Invented the Personal Computer, Co-founded Apple, and Had Fun Doing It.* New York: Norton, 2006. 191.

4. *Triumph of the Nerds: The Rise of Accidental Empires.* writ. & prod. Robert X. Cringely, perf. Steve Jobs, Steve Wozniak, Bill Gates et al. BBC, 1996.

SOURCE NOTES CONTINUED

Chapter 6. Problems in Paradise
1. Trip Hawkins. "Quotes." Graphical User Interface Gallery Guidebook. 22 Jan. 2005. 9 Apr. 2007 <www.guidebookgallery. org/extras/spotlights/lisa/quotes>.
2. Robert Slater. *Portraits in Silicon*. Cambridge, MA: MIT, 1987. 317.
3. Jeffrey S. Young & William L. Simon. *iCon: Steve Jobs, The Greatest Second Act in the History of Business*. Hoboken, NJ: Wiley, 2005. 97.
4. Ibid. 93.
5. Ibid. 123.

Chapter 7. The NeXT Step
1. Michael S. Malone. *Infinite Loop: How Apple, the World's Most Insanely Great Computer Company, Went Insane*. New York: Doubleday, 1999. 379.
2. Jeffrey S. Young and William L. Simon. *iCon: Steve Jobs, The Greatest Second Act in the History of Business*. Hoboken, NJ: Wiley, 2005. 121.
3. George Gendron. "An interview with Steven Jobs, Inc.'s Entrepreneur of the Decade." *Inc. Magazine*. Apr. 1989. 12 Apr. 2007 <www.romain-moisescot.com/steve/more/interviews/html/interviewsFR.html>.
4. Steve Jobs. "Oral History." Computerworld Honors Program International Archives, 18.20 Apr. 1995. 10 Apr. 2007 <http://www.cwhonors.org/archives/histories/jobs.pdf>.
5. Alan Deutschman. *The Second Coming of Steve Jobs*. New York: Broadway, 2000. 49.
6. Ibid. 177.
7. *Triumph of the Nerds: The Rise of Accidental Empires*. writ. & prod. Robert X. Cringely, perf. Steve Jobs, Steve Wozniak, Bill Gates et al. BBC, 1996.

Chapter 8. Returning to Apple
1. Peter Burrows. "The Seed of Apple's Innovation." *Business Week*. 12 Oct. 2004. 20 Apr. 2007 <http://www.roman-moisescot.com/steve>.
2. Alan Deutschman. *The Second Coming of Steve Jobs*. New York: Broadway, 2000. 291.
3. Jeffrey S. Young and William L. Simon. *iCon: Steve Jobs, The Greatest Second Act in the History of Business*. Hoboken, NJ: Wiley, 2005. 265.
4. Tim Berners-Lee. "Answers for Young People." 24 Apr. 2007 <http://www.w3.org/People/Berners-Lee/Kids.html#What>.

5. Michael Malone. *Infinite Loop: How Apple, the World's Most Insanely Great Computer Company, Went Insane.* New York: Doubleday, 1999. 560.
6. Ibid. 517.

Chapter 9. Pixar Story
1. Jessi Hempel. "Pixar University: Thinking outside the mouse." *San Francisco Chronicle.* 4 June 2003. 18 Apr. 2007 < http://www.sfgate.com/cgi-bin/article.cgi?file=/gate/archive/2003/06/04/pixar.DTL>.
2. William C. Taylor and Polly LaBarre. "How Pixar adds a new school of thought to Disney." *New York Times.* 29 Jan. 2006. 13 Apr. 2007 <www.nytimes.com/2006/01/29/business/yourmoney/29pixar.html>.
3. Alan Deutschman. *The Second Coming of Steve Jobs.* New York: Broadway, 2000. 119.

Chapter 10. The Age of iPod
1. Jeffrey Young and William Simon. "The God of iPod," *Sydney Morning Herald.* 24 May 2005. 26 Apr. 2007 <http://www.smh.com.au/news/Next/The-god-of-iPod/2005/05/23>.
2. Steve Jobs. "Good for the Soul." Interview with Steven Levy. *Newsweek.* 16 Oct. 2006. 26 April 2007 <www.msnbc.msn.com/id/15262121/site/newsweek/page/3>.
3. Steven Levy. *The Perfect Thing: How the iPod Shuffles Commerce, Culture, and Coolness.* New York: Simon & Schuster, 2006. 211.
4. Jeffrey S. Young and William L. Simon. *iCon: Steve Jobs, The Greatest Second Act in the History of Business.* Hoboken, NJ: Wiley, 2005. 289.
5. Charles Arthur. "Technology Special: The guru: Steve Jobs." *The Independent* (London, England). 29 Oct. 2005. 3 May 2007 <http://www.highbeam.com/DocPrint.aspx?DocId=1G1:138078590>.

INDEX

ABOUT THE AUTHOR

Scott Gillam is a former English teacher and editor of social studies and language arts textbooks. A graduate of Haverford College, he has an MA from the University of Pennsylvania and served as an education officer with the Peace Corps in Kenya. He is also the author of *Discrimination*; *Top Careers in Two Years*; *Food, Agriculture, and Natural Resources*; and *Civil Liberties*. He lives in New York City.

PHOTO CREDITS

Kim Kulish/Corbis, cover, 3; Paul Sakuma/AP Images, 6, 8, 13, 38, 46, 55, 75, 76, 95, 98 (bottom); Scott Anger/AP Images, 14; Hewlett Packard Company/AP Images, 21; Wally Fong/AP Images, 22; Kodiak Daily Mirror, Drew Herman/AP Images, 26; Saurabh Das/AP Images, 29; Heinz Nixdorf Museumsforum/AP Images, 30, 97 (top); Olivier Maire/Keystone/AP Images, 37; Apple Computers Inc./AP Images, 45, 96; AP Images, 49; Sal Veder/AP Images, 52, 97 (bottom); Richard Drew/AP Images, 56, 98 (top); NEXT, Doug Menuez/AP Images, 60; Eric Risberg/AP Images, 65, 66; Ben Margot/AP Images, 70; Bebeto Matthews/AP Images, 72; Randi Lynn Beach/AP Images, 85; Marcio Jose Sanchez/AP Images, 86, 99; Jeff Chiu/AP Images, 91